Frontier America

Volume 1

A New World

David M. Brownstone   Irene M. Franck

GROLIER

An Imprint of Scholastic Library Publishing
Danbury, Connecticut

About This Set

Frontier America is a 10-volume history of the many frontiers that together make up the earliest settled regions of what is now the United States, from the first contacts between Europeans and Native Americans to the closing of the frontier in the late 1800s.

Volumes 1 and 2 tell the story of the American frontier in a single narrative. Volume 2 also contains Highlights of American Frontier History, briefly laying out the key events in chronological order. Also in Volume 2 is a two-page map of the lower 48 states. Other smaller maps are listed at the end of the Contents page in each volume.

Volumes 3 through 10 contain a series of articles on the American frontier arranged in A–Z order. Many articles contain cross-references to other related articles. These are signaled by the use of small capital letters, like these: TEXAS LONGHORN.

The frontier period for each of the 50 states is covered in a separate article. Each state article is accompanied by a Quick Frontier Facts box, giving ready-reference highlights of that state's early frontier history.

Special longer articles are also included in Volumes 3 through 10, such as those on the Oregon-California Trail and Women on the Frontier. Such articles are indicated in red type on each volume's Contents page. They are also printed on a gold background to highlight them.

Volume 10 includes two lists of sources for more information, On the Internet and In Print, as well as image credits and acknowledgments.

Finally, each volume ends with a Set Index covering all 10 volumes. Using this, readers can easily find what they want starting from any volume. ❖

Published 2004 by Grolier,
An imprint of Scholastic Library Publishing
Old Sherman Turnpike
Danbury, Connecticut 06816

Illustration credits for all 10 volumes of *Frontier America* on pp. 87–88 of Vol. 10.

Library of Congress Cataloging-in-Publication Data

Brownstone, David M.
    Frontier America / David M. Brownstone and Irene M. Franck.
        p. cm.
    Includes bibliographic references and index.
        Contents: v. 1. A new world -- v. 2. West to the Pacific -- v. 3. Acadia—Butterfield Overland Stage -- v. 4. Cabeza de Vaca—Custer -- v. 5. Delaware—Homestead Act -- v. 6. Horses—Louisiana Purchase -- v. 7. Mail—Northwest Territory -- v. 8. Oakley—Roanoke Island -- v. 9. Rocky Mountains—Turnpike -- v. 10. Utah—Young.
        ISBN 0-7172-5990-0 (alk. paper)
        1. United States--History--Encyclopedias, Juvenile. 2. Frontier and pioneer life--United States--Encyclopedias, Juvenile. I. Franck, Irene M. II. Title.

E178.3.F825 2004
973--dc22

                                                                                        2004042445

Printed in the United States of America
Designed by K & P Publishing Services

Contents

This map, drawn by Gerardus Mercator, shows North and South America as they were known in the 1500s and labels the various regions claimed or settled by Europeans at that time.

American Frontiers

The American frontier began as many different frontiers, all formed by the meeting of invading Europeans from many countries and hundreds of Native-American peoples. In those parts of North America that became the United States, the American frontier became an ever-moving, four-centuries-long body of battle lines and settlements. In the end these covered what became the whole country, all the way from the Atlantic to the Pacific and from the Gulf of Mexico to the Canadian border. Before the American frontier closed, it also included Alaska.

At its widest the story of the American frontier is part of the story of the European invasion and conquest of the Americas. These were, in turn, part of the European attack on and partial conquest of most of the rest of the world.

For the first three of the four centuries—from the early 1500s until the end of the American Revolution late in the 1700s—the development of the North American frontiers was very much an extension of worldwide European rivalries and almost continuous wars. These American frontiers were, in effect, European colonial frontiers. At the same time, the American frontiers were also battle zones where the Native-American peoples faced the European invaders and were defeated and expelled from their homelands.

There were, of course, thousands of purely Native-American frontiers in what became the United States. Some of these battle zones went back thousands of years. Many of these frontiers were greatly affected by the tremendous changes in Native-American life and settlement stemming from the European and later American conquest. They are also part of the story of the American frontier, though in this work we will be focusing on the European–Native-American frontiers.

Throughout the New World, on land and sea, Europeans fought each other for the riches of the Americas. This is an attack on a Spanish galleon, which carried gold, silver, pearls, and other riches back to Europe.

After the American Revolution, in the parts of North America that became the United States, the European invasion and conquest changed mainly into the story of the tremendously powerful American drive west to the Pacific. That drive west was a main strand in the history of the new American nation. Along with it came the much faster defeat and expulsion of the Native-American peoples, which was another main strand in American history.

In this period after the Revolution, the new American nation defeated or bought out all of its remaining colonial rivals. In the process the Americans bought the huge territories held by France, took more than half of Mexico, and pushed Spain and Russia out of North America. ❖

Wherever European explorers went in North America, they were met by Native Americans. This painting by J. A. Théodore Gudin shows a French party under Jacques Cartier heading up the St. Lawrence River in 1535, with Native Americans watching them from the shore.

The people who arrived from Asia during the Ice Age developed techniques for living in cold climates. Their clothes, transportation, hunting practices, food sources, and much more were suited to the time and place. Some peoples still live in traditional ways, such as these Native Americans paddling kayaks in water surrounded by icebergs and glaciers, as painted by a modern artist.

The Native Americans

People settled very late in the Americas. In the Old World—Africa, Asia, and Europe—human ancestors have been found at least 4 million to 5 million years old, probably going back to prehuman origins in Africa. In the "New World" of the Americas, however, people began to arrive at the earliest 50,000 to 70,000 years ago. They emigrated as fully formed humans (*Homo sapiens*) from other parts of the world.

The first humans probably came to the Americas from Asia. They were the ancestors of the Native Americans, who might just as easily be called the "First Americans." Early European explorers arriving in the Americas mistakenly called them "Indians," for they thought they had discovered India, not realizing that Asia was still half a world away. Native Americans are still so widely called Indians that both names remain in use.

When the first humans arrived in the

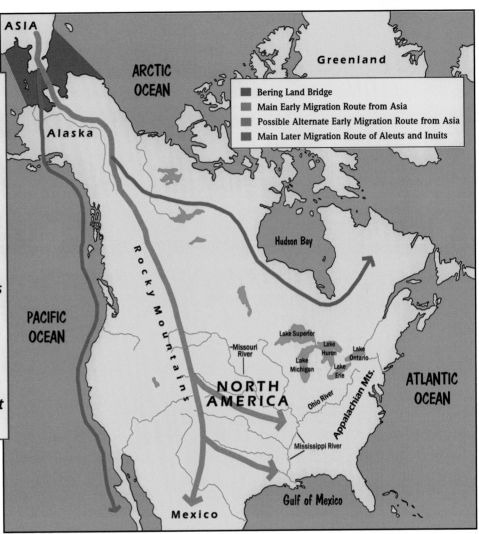

Major Early Migration Routes from Asia into North America

The main migration from Asia to North America is believed to have crossed the Bering Land Bridge during the last Ice Age, about 14,000 to 16,000 years ago. Some migrants may also have followed a route down the west coast of North America. Aleuts and Inuits arrived some thousands of years later, following a different route.

Americas—and even whether or not they really came from Asia—is a matter of much argument. Some archaeologists and historians insist that archaeological sites dating back 40,000 to 70,000 years prove that Asians began crossing Bering Strait, between northern Russia and Alaska, as much as 70,000 years ago. A few others insist that the earliest Americans came just as early as that, but by boat across the South Pacific to land on the west coast of South America.

Reliable proof of these early arrivals is small. As a result, most archaeologists and historians believe that the earliest Native Americans were northeast Asians, and that they arrived 14,000 to 16,000 years ago, crossing what was then the dry land of the Bering Land Bridge, where the water of Bering Strait now flows.

In that very cold period, glaciers covered much of the northern hemisphere. Large amounts of the earth's water were stored in these huge sheets of ice, which brought down sea levels. As a result, dry land emerged under what is now the Bering Strait waterway. It remained dry land for

The main migration of people from Asia to North America is believed to have taken place during the last major Ice Age, probably between 14,000 and 16,000 years ago. In that period much northern land was covered by vast glaciers, like this modern one in Alaska. Because these glaciers were so thick and held so much water, the sea level was much lower than it is today. As a result, territory now under water became dry land, making a pathway into North America (see map on page 9).

several thousand years, creating the main migration route for northeast Asian peoples moving into the Americas.

The first wave of Asian migration is believed to have moved across the Bering Land Bridge 14,000 to 16,000 years ago. These were the ancestors of the main body of Native-American peoples. A second but smaller wave of migrants came several thousand years later, either by way of the land bridge or by boats moving along the Aleutian Islands and the Alaska coast. These were the ancestors of the Inuit and Aleut peoples of far northern North America.

Both waves of early immigrants were

While glaciers covered much of the land, locking up water and lowering the sea level, some areas were largely ice-free. Among them were valleys in Alaska's Brooks Range, like that seen in the background here, which acted as pathways for newcomers arriving from Asia.

hunting peoples, for farming came only later in their history. They were following the migration of the reindeer, mammoths, and other animals they hunted for food. The Bering Land Bridge lasted until approximately 10,000 years ago. At that time the glacial period called the Wisconsin Glaciation brought warming and massive ice melting, causing the northern seas to rise hundreds of feet.

From those early Asian immigrants developed a hemisphere-wide population of tens of millions of Native Americans and thousands of Native-American peoples. Although no hard figures are available, the population of the Americas probably numbered 25 million to 50 million in 1492, the year Christopher Columbus and his ships arrived in the Caribbean, and the European conquest of the Americas began.

Of those, an estimated one million to three million Native Americans lived in what would later become the United States. They were organized into at least 60 major groups of peoples and 200 tribes within those groups. They spoke 10 to 12 different families of Native-American languages, with tribes and groups of tribes speaking variations of those languages.

The Native-American peoples, including those living within what became the United States, had histories, religions, and full-scale cultures stretching back thousands of years. Some Native-American peoples were still mainly hunters, but a great many were by then farmers who lived in towns. Hunters or farmers, they were part of complex, fully formed societies much like those found in many other parts of the world. Many were part of continent-wide trading networks, and all had their own well-established religions.

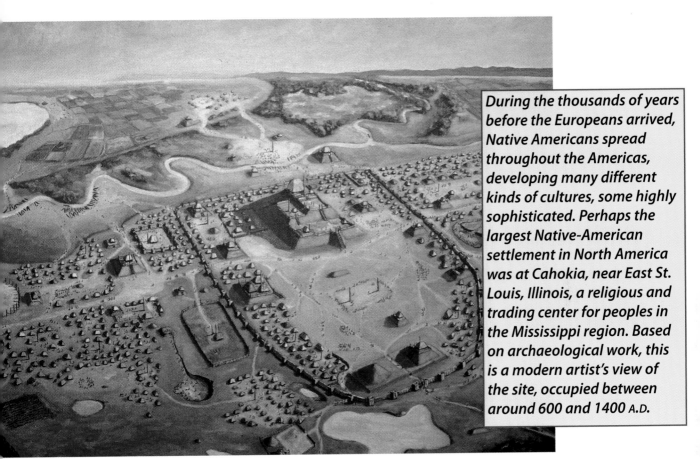

During the thousands of years before the Europeans arrived, Native Americans spread throughout the Americas, developing many different kinds of cultures, some highly sophisticated. Perhaps the largest Native-American settlement in North America was at Cahokia, near East St. Louis, Illinois, a religious and trading center for peoples in the Mississippi region. Based on archaeological work, this is a modern artist's view of the site, occupied between around 600 and 1400 A.D.

They were certainly not "savages," as many of the invading Europeans called them. Far from it. Many Native-American cultures were, in fact, at least as old as those of the Europeans who conquered them. Their great misfortune was that they had neither the weapons nor the organization they needed to successfully resist the European invaders. Equally disastrous, their bodies had no immunity (natural resistance) to the infectious diseases carried by the Europeans. Millions of Native Americans died in epidemics of these European-borne diseases. ❖

Native Americans in North America in 1492

Over thousands of years Native Americans spread out to cover the continent of North America, forming many different nations and confederations. These peoples did not simply settle in one place and stay there. Instead, as peoples around the world have always done, they migrated, fought wars, moved into new territories, and pushed previous inhabitants into other regions. This map (left) shows the approximate locations of the main Native-American peoples at the time when Columbus and other Europeans began to arrive in the Americas.

These Chinese ships (junks) were photographed at sea off Hong Kong. Some people believe that Chinese explorers sailing ships like these reached North America as early as the 500s A.D. However, if they did, they left no clear traces and established no frontier in America.

Early Voyagers

Thousands of years later some other voyagers may have traveled to the Americas. There are certainly a good many stories about early visitors from China, Egypt, Phoenicia, and several other Old World countries. For example, *The Great Chinese Encyclopedia,* a major work of Chinese scholarship published in the sixth century A.D., tells in detail of the transpacific voyage of Hui Shen's party of Chinese Buddhist priests, who reportedly landed on the west coast of North America. From there, they reportedly traveled south to a country they called *Fusang,* perhaps to what is now Mexico.

Almost a thousand years earlier, in the fourth century B.C., the Greek sailor Pytheas reportedly sailed across the Mediterranean far into the North Atlantic. According to the Roman historian Pliny,

We do not know when European sailors first ventured out into the North Atlantic. However, they probably arrived in Iceland by the 500s A.D. and perhaps much earlier, despite the danger of icebergs, like these off the coast of modern Greenland, only 200 miles west of Iceland.

Pytheas reached a land he called *Ultima Thule,* which may have been the North Atlantic island of Iceland—or perhaps even Greenland, a huge island off the northeastern coast of North America. Among the many other reports of Old World visitors to the Americas are stories of blond, blue-eyed visitors to Mexico and Peru, who some people think may have been Europeans. Some also believe that others visited the Americas long before Columbus, among them Druids, Celts from Spain, Jews, Romans, Arabs, and West Africans.

Some of these tales of ancient visitors are extremely hard to take seriously. Yet some may, in the long run, turn out to be true—and most of them are fun and fascinating. However, most of these early visitors—if they came—left little or no convincing evidence of their journeys. Nor did they leave convincing evidence of permanent settlement, making little or no imprint on the history of the Americas.

The North Atlantic was the main seaway used by early European sailors and settlers headed west to the Americas. By the third and fourth centuries B.C. a strong warming trend had started in the waters of the North Atlantic. This melted a great deal of the ice that before then had largely barred the way west. Phoenician and Greek sailors, such as Pytheas (see p. 14), may have reached the North Atlantic as early as the fourth century B.C. More surely we know that Irish sea rovers had reached and started to settle the string of islands stretching across the North Atlantic as early as the 500s A.D. They probably reached and settled in Iceland, only 200 miles east of Greenland.

The Norse Settlements

This replica of a Viking ship sailed off Newfoundland's Norse settlement, L'Anse aux Meadows, in July 2000, celebrating the 1,000th anniversary of Leif Eriksson's voyage to North America. The ship was named the Snorri, after the first Norse child known to have been born in North America.

The first Europeans who certainly reached and settled in North America were the Norse (Vikings from Norway). In the process they created the first Native-American–European frontier. By the seventh century A.D. the Norse had settled in northern Scotland and northern Ireland, and had moved west into the Shetland Islands and the Faeroe Islands. In the mid–ninth century A.D. Norse ships reached Iceland. By 900 A.D. the Norse population of Iceland was an estimated 20,000, reaching an estimated 40,000 in 930 A.D.

In the early 980s Erik the Red founded the first known Norse settlement, called the Eastern Settlement, in Greenland. His story is told in the Icelandic *Saga of Erik the Red*. Leif Eriksson, his son, was among those Greenlanders believed to have later landed and established settlements in Newfoundland in far northeastern North America. The oldest European settlement so far found on the North American mainland is the Norse settlement at L'Anse aux

Leif Eriksson is shown here arriving in America in about 1000 A.D. The painting, which hangs in the United States Capitol, is Per Krohg's copy of an 1893 painting by his father Christian Krohg, celebrating that event.

Meadows, on the northern tip of Newfoundland, which is now a Canadian National Historic Site and a World Historic Site.

The Norse settlement in Greenland lasted for at least 500 years, perhaps even until after the Columbus "discovery" of America in 1492. In some periods the Norse population of Greenland reached 5,000 to 10,000. It ended largely because the long warm spell in the North Atlantic gave way to a much colder period called the "Little Ice Age." Then massive ice floes blocked the North Atlantic shipping lanes to and from Iceland and Europe.

We know little or nothing about Greenland's Native-American peoples, whom the Norse called *Skrellings* or *Skraelings*. We do know that, from the first, the Norse settlers and those Native Americans were in con-

They went ashore and looked about them. The weather was fine. There was dew on the grass. . . . There was no lack of salmon in the river or the lake, bigger salmon than they had ever seen. The country seemed to them so kind that no winter fodder would be needed for livestock: there was never any frost all winter and the grass hardly withered at all. . . .

Description of the place named Vinland, possibly in North America, from Iceland's *Saga of Erik the Red*

flict. In one sense their long conflict was a model of much that was to come during the later full-scale European invasion and conquest of the Americas. In another sense, though, it was very different, for in Greenland the Europeans finally abandoned their settlements, returning to Iceland.

Yet, even while the Norse Greenland colonies were in the process of failing, the main European invasion of the Americas began. In the North Atlantic this westward move was probably aided by Portuguese, British, Basque, and Breton (French) seafarers. They had fished on the Grand Banks, off Newfoundland, from the mid-1400s, and many had landed on the Newfoundland shore to dry their fish and trade with local Native Americans. ❖

About a thousand years ago, some 500 years before Columbus, Norse immigrants from northern Europe lived in huts like these reconstructed at L'Anse aux Meadows on the coast of Newfoundland. However, as the climate later grew much colder, they left their North American settlements.

The Pinta, the Niña, and the Santa Maria carried Italian sailor Christopher Columbus and his Spanish expedition across the Atlantic in 1492, he thought to Asia, but actually to the Americas.

The European Invasion

The European invasion and conquest of the Americas (and much of the rest of the world) began with one of the greatest of all European defeats, almost half the world away. In 1453 the Ottoman Turks took Constantinople (later Istanbul), in what is now Turkey, and blocked east–west trade through that city, which had been the most important gateway between Europe and Asia for thousands of years.

European trading nations, especially Portugal and Spain, had already been seeking new trading routes to the East. After Constantinople fell in 1453, they greatly speeded up that search. In the 1480s and 1490s their search bore fruit. Portuguese ships rounded Africa's Cape of Good Hope in 1487, entering the Indian Ocean. Portugal's Vasco da Gama reached and attacked Indian ports in 1498. The long

European attack on southern and eastern Asia had begun.

Spanish and Portuguese ships also sailed west, across the Atlantic. The first to arrive were the Spanish ships *Niña, Pinta,* and *Santa María,* led by Italian navigator Christopher Columbus. On October 12, 1492, the Columbus expedition reached the Caribbean island of San Salvador, also called Watling Island or Guanahani. This signaled the beginning of the European conquest of the Americas and of what would become a huge Spanish-American colonial empire. On the island of Hispaniola, which the Spanish called Santo Domingo, Columbus founded Navidad, the first Spanish (and European) base in the Americas. Columbus made three voyages to the Americas (1492, 1493, and 1498), exploring and claiming for Spain much of the Caribbean and the northeast coast of South America.

On Hispaniola Columbus began the centuries-long history of the enslavement and often destruction of the Native-American peoples of the Americas. When Columbus arrived, Hispaniola was the homeland of the Taino people, with a population estimated at one million. On returning to Spain after his first voyage, Columbus took four enslaved Tainos with him from Hispaniola. In 1494 a Taino rebellion against the Spanish invaders failed, and Columbus sent hundreds of Taino slaves back to Spain. By the 1530s epidemic diseases, forced labor in slavery, and war had reduced the Tainos to

Thirty-three days after my departure [from Spain] I reached the Indian Sea, where I discovered many islands, thickly peopled, of which I took possession without resistance in the name of our most illustrious monarch, by public proclamation and with unfurled banners. To the first of these islands, which is called by the Indians Guanahani, I gave the name of the blessed Savior (San Salvador), relying upon whose protection I had reached this as well as the other islands. . . .

From a letter by Christopher Columbus, dated March 14, 1493, about the events of October 12, 1492

Columbus's first landfall in the Americas is believed to have been on the Caribbean island of San Salvador, originally called Guanahani and later Watling's Island. That event took place on October 12, 1492.

only a few thousand people. The same fate was soon suffered by other Native-American peoples throughout the Caribbean, part of the huge losses suffered by Native-Americans throughout the Americas.

Hispaniola also saw the beginning of African-American slavery in the Americas. In 1501 the first Black African slaves in the Americas were brought to Hispaniola. They were imported at the start partly to replace the many enslaved Native-American workers who had been killed or died of disease or overwork.

In 1500, eight years after the first Columbus voyage, Pedro Cabral's Portuguese expedition landed on the South American mainland in what would become Portuguese Brazil, the largest country in South America. Portugal and Spain had earlier agreed to peacefully split the colonial world into Portuguese and Spanish sections. Under the terms of the Treaty of Tordesillas (1494), Portugal's American empire was largely limited to Brazil, while Spain was free to develop what became its enormous empire in the Americas. In return, Spain stayed out of Africa and Asia, allowing Portugal to develop its own huge eastern empire, from Africa to the Far East.

Other European explorers and conquerors also arrived in the Americas, though widespread settlement and the establishment of European–Native-American frontiers did not begin until the mid-1500s. In 1497 Italian sailor John Cabot (born Giovanni Caboto) led his English ship across the North Atlantic to Newfoundland. He was the first of the new European explorers to land in North America, claiming the region for England.

Twelve years later, in 1509, his son Sebastian Cabot sailed his English ship farther, almost finding the way into Hudson Bay and the heart of the North American continent. Still another English expedition, this one led by Italian sailor Giovanni da Verrazzano, explored the North American coast as far south as New England and New York in 1524.

The French arrived in 1534 and 1535, with Jacques Cartier's voyages deep into North America. Cartier's expedition traveled on the St. Lawrence River all the way to what would become the Canadian cities of Quebec and Montreal.

John Cabot established English claims to North America when he landed on the shores of northeastern Canada in 1497, though we do not know exactly where. Sailing for the English, Cabot was born in Italy as Giovanni Caboto.

Early Colonial Frontiers

During the 1500s and 1600s, six European nations established colonies—and therefore frontier regions—in those parts of North America that later became the United States. Three of them—Britain, France, and Spain—became the leading contenders in a long series of conflicts over North America. Two others—the Netherlands and Sweden —developed but lost colonies on the Atlantic coast of North America.

The sixth nation, Russia, expanded east across Asia and then moved across the Bering Strait to occupy Alaska. Russia later moved south on the Pacific coast, until confronted by the power of the new United States after the American Revolution.❖

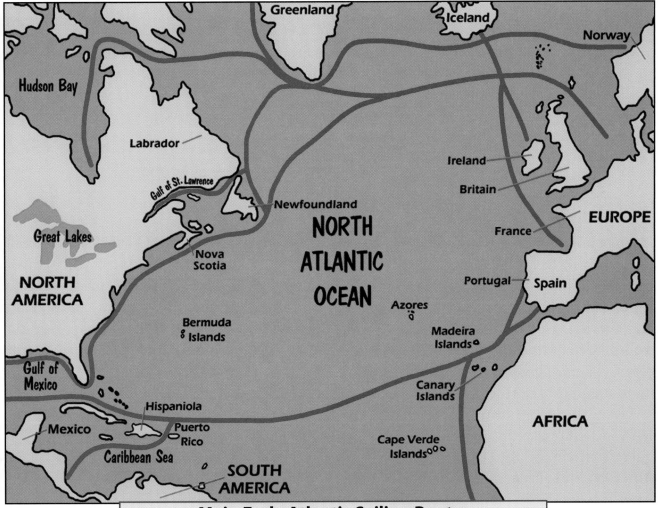

Main Early Atlantic Sailing Routes
Most early European visitors to North America came by the North Atlantic sailing routes. Columbus and most Spanish ships took a more southerly route across to the Caribbean and farther south.

Native Americans rightly feared the Spanish invaders in the Caribbean and the Gulf of Mexico. This 1518 manuscript shows a Native American (in tree) spying on a Spanish ship off the Mexican coast, with a sailor in a small boat fishing for fresh food.

Spanish America

Spain's huge American empire stretched all the way from Tierra del Fuego, on the southern tip of South America, to California, the American Southwest, the Mississippi Valley, and Florida. However, its territory in what would become the United States consisted of only some lightly settled border regions on that empire's northern fringe.

After the Columbus voyages of the 1490s, Spain rapidly attacked and conquered much of the Caribbean, Central America, and the northern parts of South America. By 1515 Spanish forces had taken Puerto Rico and Cuba, and they were using Cuba as a base for exploring the Central American and South American mainlands.

In 1519 Hernando Cortés led a small Spanish force, with thousands of Native-American allies, against the massive Aztec Empire, defeating the Aztecs and taking Mexico. Spain was then able to expand north farther into North America and south into Central America. In 1532 Francisco Pizarro led a Spanish force of only 200 against Peru's Inca Empire. Within two years Spain had defeated the Incas, and it soon established control of much of South America.

In the 1520s and 1530s Spanish explorers, soldiers, and settlers began moving into the territories that would later become the United States—though the first permanent

Early Spanish forces used Native-American rivalries to advance their conquests. After Cortés arrived in Mexico, as shown here in an image from about 1550, the Spanish defeated the nation of Tlaxcala, which then joined in the Spanish attack on the Aztecs.

Spanish settlement, at St. Augustine, Florida, would not be established until 1565.

Spanish explorer Juan Ponce de León led two expeditions to Florida, in 1513 and 1521. Both were aimed at conquest, though some stories have included his search for a mythical "Fountain of Youth." On the west Florida coast he encountered Native-American peoples who had earlier met and fought Spanish slavers. They in no way wel-comed Ponce de León. His first invasion attempt, in 1513, was defeated by the local Calusas, who drove off his ships before they reached land. His second, in 1521, was also defeated by the Calusas, who again drove off the Spanish invaders. This time Ponce de León was seriously wounded and died of his wounds after retreating to Cuba.

Native-American peoples on the north-ern frontiers of Spain's huge American

Spanish forces under Hernando de Soto pushed their way through much of southeastern North America, starting in 1539 with his landing in Florida (shown here). By 1541 they reached the Mississippi River, where de Soto died of disease a year later.

empire threw back many other Spanish raiding and colonizing parties during the 1500s. One of the largest failed colonizing parties was that of Pánfilo de Narváez. In 1528 he led a 400-strong expedition to what is now Tampa, on the west coast of Florida. After landing, the Narváez party was forced by the Apalachee and other local Native-American peoples to fight its way northwest along the coast of the Gulf of Mexico. Defeated by Apalachee bowmen, Narváez fled along the Gulf Coast in hastily built boats. The Narváez party came to rest with fewer than one hundred survivors in Galveston Bay, on the east Texas coast. In 1536 four survivors reached Mexico City.

Another major failed expedition was that of Hernando de Soto, who landed on the west coast of Florida at the head of a 600-strong Spanish armed force in May 1539. In the four years that followed, de Soto's forces suffered several major defeats as they fought and looted their way from Florida through the Southeast and Mid-South in a wholly unsuccessful search for gold and other treasures. De Soto reached the Mississippi River in 1541 and died there of disease in May 1542. The remnants of his force survived by sailing south on the Mississippi to the Gulf of Mexico. Among de Soto's major Native-American opponents were the Apalachee, Chickasaw, and Natchez peoples.

From the start of their invasion of the Americas, the Spanish attacked Native Americans, conquering and killing many, and effectively enslaving many of the survivors. This image from about 1550 shows such events taking place after Cortés's arrival on the east coast of Mexico, near what is now Veracruz.

De Soto and his party brought with them diseases the Spanish had unwittingly carried from Europe. Because these diseases were not known in the Americas, the Native-American peoples had no resistance to them. Many Native-American peoples were largely destroyed.

An even larger Spanish expedition was that of Francisco Vásquez de Coronado. He led his forces north out of Mexico into Pueblo Native-American country in the Southwest in 1540, reaching the Grand Canyon of the Colorado River. Before retreating to Mexico in 1542, Coronado's well-armed forces briefly took Zuni Pueblo and several other pueblos (towns). Like de Soto, Coronado found none of the gold and

This is a typical Spanish conquistador in armor on horseback in New Spain in the 1500s.

other treasures they had sought. However, Coronado did bring with him a change with far-reaching results: He introduced the horse, which would vastly change the lives and cultures of the Native Americans of the West and Southwest.

Farther west, in 1542–1543, Juan Cabrillo's Spanish ships explored the west coast of North America from central Mexico to Oregon. These explorations pointed the way to the later establishment of Spain's California frontier.

Spain's Florida Frontier

The first permanent Spanish settlement in North America—and the first permanent European settlement in what would become the United States—was established at St. Augustine, Florida, in 1565 by Pedro Menéndez de Avilés. Two years earlier, in 1563, French Huguenots had founded several settlements in South Carolina and Florida, including Fort Caroline, at the mouth of Florida's St. Johns River. Spanish forces, pushing north in Florida, responded by attacking and destroying the French settlements, including Fort Caroline. Mirroring the Protestant-Catholic civil wars that were sweeping Europe in that period, the Catholic

Spanish killed hundreds of the Protestant French Huguenots for the "crime" of heresy (differing religious beliefs).

As governor of Spain's Florida colony, Menéndez moved to expand the colony far beyond St. Augustine. Spanish soldiers, often accompanied by Catholic priests, explored and set up outposts on the coast as far north as Chesapeake Bay and south-

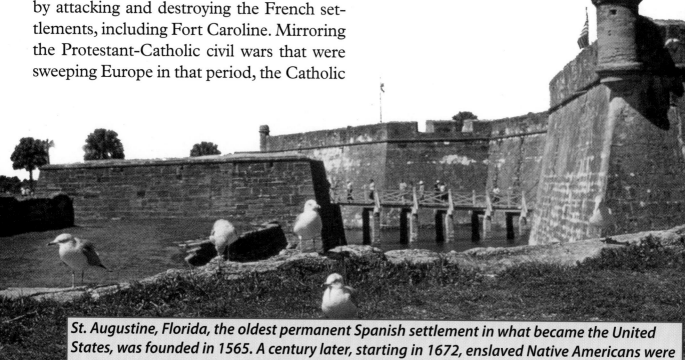

St. Augustine, Florida, the oldest permanent Spanish settlement in what became the United States, was founded in 1565. A century later, starting in 1672, enslaved Native Americans were used to build the massive fort called Castillo de San Marcos, parts of which survive.

Near the site of Fort Caroline, on the St. Johns River in Florida, modern archaeologists have reconstructed shelters made of palm fronds, like those used by early Native Americans in the region, the Timucua.

ern Virginia. Some of the Spanish also went west, establishing outposts deep into the South. Many followed de Soto's path west and met the same kind of Native-American resistance that had defeated de Soto. Throughout the region, Spanish priests, soldiers, and settlers fought and often enslaved Native-American peoples, who fought back and in this period defeated the Spanish.

Spain's problems were not confined to its Native-American wars. Just as Spain had made war on the French Huguenots, so other European powers made war on Spain. The English, engaged in a massive war with Spain in Europe, took note of Spanish expansion north in the Americas

and attacked on Spain's East Coast frontier. In 1586 Francis Drake's ships, en route home after attacking Spanish Caribbean colonies and treasure ships, stopped to attack and burn St. Augustine. After that attack St. Augustine was rebuilt. However, by 1600 it was the only substantial Spanish settlement left in Florida.

This Spanish coat of arms was built into the wall of the Castillo San Marcos, the fort that guarded St. Augustine, Florida, begun in 1672.

New Mexico

Spain's second permanent colony in what would become the United States—the colony of Nuevo (New) Mexico in the American Southwest—proved far sturdier than its Florida settlements. However, Spain's northern frontiers in the New World, which came to stretch all the way from Florida to California and included all of northern Mexico, continued to be frontier areas. Never fully in Spanish control, these frontier regions were always beset by Native-American resistance and European and American opponents.

When Spanish explorers first arrived in the Southwest, they introduced horses, previously unknown in the region. Navajo artists depicted their arrival in these pictures on a rock face in the Canyon de Chelly area of Arizona.

From the days of the de Soto and Coronado expeditions of the 1500s to the Mexican-American Wars of the 1840s, Spanish North America was under attack by competitors. These attacks, mainly by the

One of the most influential Spanish expeditions into the American Southwest was that led by Francisco de Coronado in the early 1540s. It introduced the horse to the heart of North America, forever changing the Native-American culture there. This Frederic Remington image shows the expedition crossing New Mexico.

The San Miguel Mission in Santa Fe, New Mexico, dates back to 1610, only a dozen years after Juan de Oñate led a group of Spanish settlers north to found the city. Rebuilt in 1710, it is the oldest surviving church in the United States.

British, French, and Americans, were part of a worldwide set of colonial wars. At the same time, they were accompanied by widespread Native-American resistance. The result was an ever-shifting set of alliances between various Native-American nations and the colonial powers. Only when the colonial wars ended, in the 19th century, would the conflicts in the Spanish and Mexican borderland frontiers end.

The first successful Spanish expedition into the Southwest came in 1598. Juan de Oñate led a 200-strong party of soldiers, settlers, and Catholic missionary priests, with 100 wagons and 7,000 head of livestock. They traveled north out of Mexico City into Mexico's wild northern frontier region by way of central Mexico's Camino Real (Royal Road). Two months later, the party reached the Rio Grande (Río Bravo or Rapid River of the North), crossing at El Paso (The Pass) into what would become the United States. The northern part of Oñate's route would later be known as the Chihuahua Trail. At the Rio Grande, Oñate claimed the entire region for Spain and named himself its governor. The expedition did not find the rich silver mines sought by

Native-American traditions survive in many parts of the American Southwest. These are Native-American dancers in traditional costume performing in modern New Mexico.

Spain, and Oñate was later replaced. However, the colony continued, with its capital city becoming Santa Fe (Holy Faith), in what is now northern New Mexico.

The New Mexico colony did not flourish in the decades that followed, but it did survive. Its trade was controlled out of distant Mexico City. For many kinds of goods it depended on a caravan from Mexico City, which was scheduled for every three years but was often delayed. The Spanish clergy converted and effectively enslaved large numbers of the peaceful Pueblo peoples of the area, punishing them harshly when they tried to resume their own religions.

Spanish colonists remained in a very nearly constant state of war with many sharply resistant and warlike Native-American peoples in northern Mexico and to the north and east of the New Mexico colony. From the Conquest of the early 1500s into the early 1900s, Yaqui forces in northern Mexico fought Spain and later independent Mexico again and again. In what became the American Southwest, Apaches and Comanches led armed Native-American resistance against Spanish, Mexican, and then United States rule far into the 19th century.

Under a leader named Popé, the Pueblo peoples retook New Mexico in 1680. Four hundred Spanish settlers were killed in this Pueblo Revolt. The remaining 2,200 fled, most of them to the El Paso area. Yet the revolt was short-lived. Spanish forces retook the colony in 1692 and quickly reoccupied it, mostly with settlers who had fled 12 years earlier.

Spain would then hold New Mexico until Mexico won its independence in 1821. The region remained a frontier region, however. Although the Pueblos never again retook their territories, the Yaquis, Apaches, Comanches, and several other Native-American peoples of the Southwest continued their fierce resistance.

Other Spanish-American Frontiers

Beyond Florida and New Mexico, most of Spain's other far northern frontiers were little more than lightly settled, largely unconquered frontier areas, the homelands of many Native-American nations. These included California, Texas, the Gulf Coast, and the southern Mississippi Valley. These regions gained little attention from Spain itself or from Mexico City, the center of Spanish colonial power in North America. These regions were also claimed by other European powers—England to the east; France in Texas, the Gulf Coast, and the Mississippi Valley; and Russia in California.

Reflecting the lack of colonial attention, Spain did not even begin to settle huge—and (as it would turn out) tremendously rich—California until the 1760s, more than 160 years after the Oñate expedition into New Mexico. Before the 1760s the Spanish made some failed attempts to move into California by land from Baja (Lower) California, but these were all thrown back by Native-American forces.

The first California mission was established by Father Junípero Serra in San Diego only in 1769. In the next half century Spanish Catholic priests and soldiers

Father Junípero Serra led the Spanish effort to colonize California, founding a series of Catholic missions along its coastline. A statue of Serra graces the garden of the first of these missions, the San Diego Mission, founded in 1769.

went on to establish a string of 21 missions, stretching from San Diego to north of San Francisco. In the process they conquered and enslaved thousands of California's Native Americans. However, Spanish settlement was very light. By 1800 California still had fewer than 1,000 Spanish settlers.

For California's Native Americans, the Spanish invasion was a disaster. As in other Spanish settlements, many Native Americans were converted and effectively enslaved. The Spanish soldiers, priests, and settlers also carried with them the same kinds of epidemic diseases that would destroy Native-American populations throughout much of North America.

In Texas many Native-American nations, led by Comanche and Apache forces, fought Spanish settlement. They strongly and successfully resisted Spanish efforts to force them to give up their own religions and

Wherever they went, Spanish colonists were accompanied by Catholic priests and established missions. This is the Mission Concepción, founded in 1740 near what is now San Antonio, Texas.

Priests and soldiers worked hand in hand in the Spanish colonies. Here Spanish priests are shown outside a California mission, with some soldiers (left) and Native-American converts (right).

become Spanish slaves. As part of that resistance, they allied themselves with France. The French supplied them with trade goods and weapons, while building their own frontier regions, especially in the Mississippi Valley. In 1790 the Spanish population of Texas was only 2,500, with most of these in San Antonio. Beyond that, the Spanish frontier in Texas was little more than a group of small outposts.

The Gulf Coast and the lower Mississippi Valley presented a similar picture. However, the Spanish faced increasing French and English strength, as well as continuing and growing Native-American resistance.

By the early 1700s Spanish settlements and influence had sharply declined in Florida and the Carolinas. English traders, colonists, and armed forces became the dominant Europeans in much of Florida, the Carolinas, and Georgia. Farther west, in the lower Mississippi Valley, French power grew to replace earlier Spanish colonial penetration. The main conflicts in the Mississippi region would be between France, Britain, and their Native-American allies. ❖

French Frontiers

Most of France's early North American explorers, traders, and soldiers came across the North Atlantic, rather than taking the Spanish southern routes across the Atlantic. For well over a century France sent very few settlers. Early French America was a very large but thinly settled trading empire, rather than a body of frontier regions like those the Spanish and British developed in North America.

In the early 1660s, as the long French-British battle for North America heated up, France began to send much larger numbers of settlers to Quebec and other areas of French Canada. However, in what became the United States, substantial French frontier regions developed only in the southern and midwestern Mississippi Valley. That is the basic reason that the French played only a small role in the history of the U.S. frontier and in U.S. history as a whole, though they played a major role in every aspect of Canadian history.

This is a modern artist's view of Jacques Cartier and other French explorers visiting the Native-American village of Hochelaga. It would later become the French city of Montreal.

The first of the great French explorers of North America was Jacques Cartier. In 1534 he followed the routes earlier taken by the fishing boats of many nations across the North Atlantic. He then went farther, sailing into the Gulf of St. Lawrence, the main northern entry into the mainland of North America. A year later, in 1535, Cartier went even farther, entering the St. Lawrence River valley, and so opening the whole North American mainland to European penetration. Cartier had found one of the only two easy, swift water routes into the heartland of North America.

Almost a century and half later, in 1677, Robert La Salle would complete the French journey into the heartland, exploring south to reach the Gulf of Mexico at the mouth of the great Mississippi River. Only a little while later, in 1700, Frenchman Pierre Le Moyne took the second main way into the North American heartland: He traveled north out of the Gulf of Mexico into the mouth of the Mississippi.

On the St. Lawrence River in 1535, Cartier's ship first reached the Native-American village of Stadacona (later the site of Quebec City) and then traveled far-

Ships could sail on the St. Lawrence River only as far as Montreal (Hochelaga). There they encountered the Lachine Rapids, a region of fast-moving, rocky waters, which could only be navigated by canoes or small flat-bottomed boats. This is Frances Anne Hopkins's 1879 painting Shooting the Rapids.

ther on the river, reaching the village of Hochelaga (later the site of Montreal). Cartier could take his ship no farther than Hochelaga, for there he encountered the Lachine Rapids, which blocked the way. No matter; by then the French had opened North America to Europe. At Montreal they were west of the Appalachian Moun-tains. That chain would for two centuries make it difficult for the British to settle in the North American heartland.

From Montreal the French were able to explore widely. They also established a huge American trading empire that reached south to New Orleans and the Gulf of Mexico, and west into the Rocky Mountains.

The Fur Trade

What the French—and later the British and Americans—primarily traded for was fur. Most desired was beaver fur, which was widely used throughout Europe and also in North America for men's hats and clothing for three centuries, from the early 1500s to the early 1900s.

In the mid-1500s North America had millions of beaver. By the early 1900s trappers and fur traders had come very close to killing the whole beaver population of the continent. They followed the ever-smaller numbers of beaver west, in the process also acting as explorers and then guides for the tide of American and Canadian settlers that followed them. Other fur-bearing animals were also hunted, including the huge numbers of sea otters killed off the Pacific coast of the continent. However, it was the hugely valuable beaver that fueled the immense and long-lasting fur trade.

From the start of French penetration into North America, the fur trade greatly influenced French–Native-American relations. For the Spanish and British in what became the United States, Native Americans were often enemies, for they resisted being expelled from their homelands by invading Europeans. However, for French fur traders, Native Americans were trading partners. Some Native-American nations served as "middlemen" in the fur trade.

They would buy furs from peoples farther inland and sell them to the French. In return they would get guns, ammunition, and other valuable European goods that Native Americans could not make for themselves.

Even before Cartier's voyages, the French and the Montagnais were trading for furs brought from far inland. Their main trading location was at the mouth of the Saguenay River, where it empties into the St. Lawrence. That pattern would be repeated for hundreds of years in Canadian and United States frontier regions. However, it was less common in the United States, where peaceful trading was often quickly overcome by war, as Native-American peoples were expelled from their homelands.

This beaver fur pelt has been stretched on a sapling frame laced with rawhide. For centuries beaver fur was sought primarily for use in making hats and other clothing.

French and other fur traders crossed the continent of North America seeking the highly prized furs of the American beaver. Hunted almost to extinction, the beaver later revived and is again widely found, like this modern beaver on top of its lodge.

This Quebec fur trader is traveling in a horse-drawn sleigh in winter, with beaver and other fur pelts hanging over the side of the sleigh, as painted in a watercolor dating from the early 1800s.

After Cartier, small numbers of French traders and farmers settled along the St. Lawrence River between Quebec City and Montreal, forming the first French North American frontier region. For more than a century the French occupied a long, thin stretch of riverfront farmland, with the river itself as their only major road.

A lively fur trade also grew. The French in Montreal traded inland for furs with the Ottawas as middlemen. The Ottawas traveled far inland in their light birchbark canoes, fit for swift passage over shallow rivers even when loaded with furs. A little farther into North America, the Hurons also became key middlemen in the French fur trade. They traded for furs with Native-American peoples out into the Great Lakes country.

The French Ways West

In the 1600s French explorers, traders, a few settlers, and some Catholic priests began moving west out of Montreal, following their Native-American trading partners as they hunted dwindling numbers of beaver. That pattern would be followed throughout Canada and the United States as long as there were fur-bearing animals to hunt.

The main French trading partners in this early period were the Hurons. This Native-American nation developed a very substantial fur-trading area of its own, stretching

In northern countries fur trappers and traders often used the kind of birchbark canoes long built by Native Americans. These were relatively light, so they could be unloaded and portaged (carried) around obstacles. The canoes could also be used as shelters in camp, as in this watercolor painted in the 1870s.

from eastern Canada far into the Midwest and the Great Lakes. The Hurons, in turn, traded with many other Native-American nations, among them the Ottawas and Ojibwas. These peoples trapped beaver, deer, and other fur-bearing animals, as well as acting as fur-trading middlemen to Native-American nations even farther west.

Some Native-American fur-trading nations, such as the Wyandots and Ottawas, migrated west, following the ever-fewer beaver. Many others, and especially the powerful Iroquois, fought for control of the fur trade, driving their defeated enemies

farther west. Late in the 1600s these wars tended to become part of the growing general French-British war over control of North America, which was itself part of a worldwide set of colonial wars between these two great European imperial nations.

One of the earliest and greatest of the French explorers and traders who opened up a huge French North American trading empire was Samuel de Champlain. In 1613 and 1615 he made historic journeys west as far as Lake Huron, deep into what is now the Canadian province of Ontario. He was followed by Étienne Brûlé, who probably

reached Lake Superior between 1615 and 1620, and Jean Nicolet. In 1634 Nicolet traveled much farther west, to Green Bay, in what is now Wisconsin, on the north shore of Lake Michigan, and then on to Lake Superior.

These French and later British explorers and traders were all pushing west on what would become the trans-Canada route. It was a British explorer, Alexander Mackenzie, who first reached the Pacific coast by land. That event, in 1793, marked a major turning point in Canadian history.

The Mississippi Valley

There was a second early French way west, which would be far more important to United States history than to Canadian history. This route followed the trans-Canada route west as far as Green Bay, before turning south and soon reaching the Wisconsin River. The Wisconsin was part of the huge Mississippi River system, which drains the whole heartland of North America. Louis Jolliet and Father Jacques Marquette took this route in 1673, going from the Wisconsin to the Mississippi near what is now Prairie du Chien, Wisconsin. Traveling on the great river in two birchbark

In 1673 Father Jacques Marquette, Louis Jolliet, and their French party were the first Europeans to venture onto the upper Mississippi River, as shown here.

canoes, they went south to the mouth of the Arkansas River before turning back, a distance of almost a thousand miles. Nine years later, in 1682, French explorer Robert La Salle would reach the mouth of the Mississippi, completing the long French journey from the Gulf of St. Lawrence to the Gulf of Mexico.

In this period the French also entered the Mississippi Valley from the south by sea. Between 1698 and 1702 they established forts at Biloxi, in what is now Mississippi, and Mobile, now in Alabama. In 1700 the French founded New Orleans, which would be the center of French power in the region for a century and a half. French set-

Father Jacques Marquette died in what is now Michigan in 1675, shortly after returning from a mission to Illinois.

tlers moved into New Orleans and the Mississippi Valley, some coming from Canada, some from French colonies in the Caribbean, and some directly from France. They also brought into Louisiana substantial numbers of African-American slaves to work in the developing plantation economy of the lower Mississippi Valley.

French settlements, some little more than forts and fur-trading posts, grew in the Mississippi Valley. They were established in many locations, among them Baton Rouge, Natchitoches, and Natchez. Farther north on the Mississippi, French posts were established at Cahokia and Kaskaskia.

Soon a three-way contest developed with the French, British, and Spanish all fighting for the southern Mississippi Valley. For France and Britain the region became part of their long struggle for dominance in North America. Although the region was contested by the Europeans, it continued to be dominated by its Native-American nations well into the 1700s. European and American colonial populations in the Mississippi region were comparatively small, while the area was home to several of the most powerful and numerous Native-American nations in North America. France's key Native-American allies against the English in their long Mississippi Valley conflict were the Choctaws, Chickasaws, and Alabamas. However, the wars of the period featured a continually shifting set of alliances between the many Native-American and European nations involved.❖

Expedition of Robert Cavelier de La Salle, *an 1844 painting by J. A. Théodore Gudin, shows the French expedition sailing on the Mississippi River in Louisiana in 1682.*

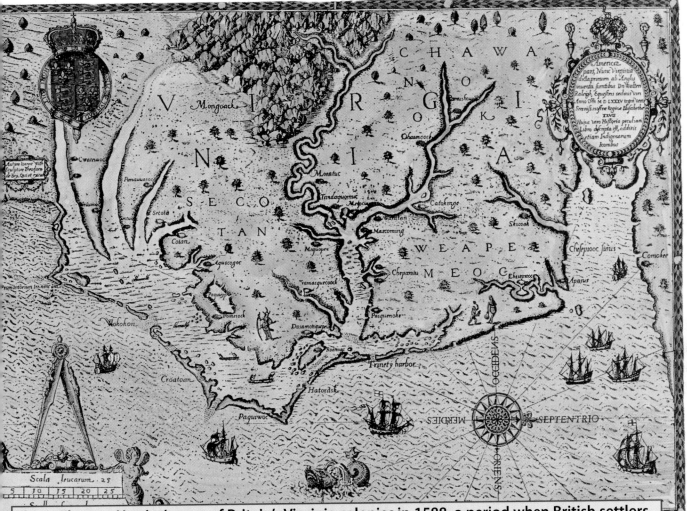

This is Thomas Harriot's map of Britain's Virginia colonies in 1588, a period when British settlers attempted to establish three colonies off what is now North Carolina, all of which failed.

British Frontiers

Many British voyages to North America followed those of John and Sebastian Cabot. Most of them were made by fishing ships to the rich Grand Banks off Newfoundland. There the British joined Portuguese, Basque, and Breton (French) ships fishing the waters, as Native Americans had long done. It was on the northeastern Atlantic shore that Native-American–European fish and fur trading had begun.

During the 1500s several notable British explorers followed the Cabots to North America. Most of them unsuccessfully sought a Northwest Passage to the Far East. As it turned out, such a passage did not exist, but it did spur exploration.

One of the earliest British explorers was Martin Frobisher. From 1576 to 1578 he led three expeditions across the North Atlantic to the far northern coast of North

America. In the process he explored the coasts of Greenland and Labrador and discovered Frobisher Bay. Another noted British explorer was John Davis. From 1585 to 1587 he explored the western coast of Greenland and the waters of what came to be called Davis Strait.

In the same period the British also became interested in developing North American colonies. Sponsored by Walter Raleigh, and with the unofficial approval of Queen Elizabeth, three attempts were made to establish a colony on Roanoke Island, off the coast of what is now North Carolina, in 1585, 1586, and 1587. The first colony failed, and the settlers were withdrawn to

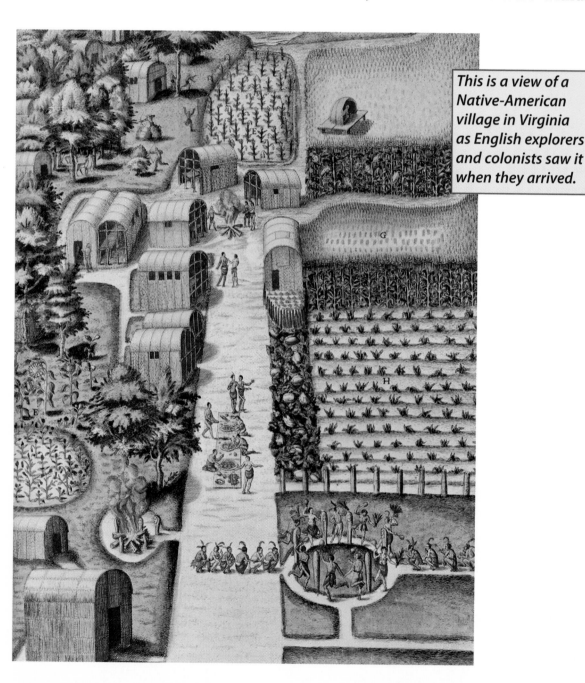

This is a view of a Native-American village in Virginia as English explorers and colonists saw it when they arrived.

An English View of the American Land

God did make the world to be inhabited by mankind, and to have his name known to all nations, and from generation to generation as the people increased and dispersed themselves into such countries as they found most convenient. And there in Florida, Virginia, New England and Canada is more land than all the people of Christendom can cultivate, and yet more to spare than all the natives of those countries can use and cultivate. And shall we here keep such a small island, and at such great rents and rates, where there is so much of the world uninhabited, and as much more in other places, and as good or rather better than any we now possess, were it cultivated and used accordingly?

From *Advertisementz for the Inexperienced Planters of New England*, by John Smith, London, 1631

Britain. The second and third disappeared, with an apparent loss of all the colonists.

Another British settlement, Popham Colony, was established by 120 British colonists in 1608 at Sagadahoc at the mouth of Maine's Kennebec River. That colony also failed, and its settlers returned to England in 1609. They had met strong resistance from the Abenakis, a group of Native-American peoples who controlled large sections of what are now northern Maine and Canada's Maritime Provinces.

Not until 1607 was Britain's first successful North American colony established, at Jamestown, Virginia. From it and the later Plymouth settlement would grow Britain's North American colonies and ultimately the United States of America.

Native-American villages in Virginia and many other parts of the Americas were often built inside protective fortifications. One common kind of fort, shown here, was protected by palisades, fences of pointed sticks (pales).

The First British Frontier

The first permanent British settlement in North America, Jamestown was established on May 13, 1607, founded by the 105 settlers who arrived on the *Sarah Constant, Goodspeed,* and *Recovery.* Of key importance for the development of North America, Jamestown opened the first British frontier region in North America, from which the first major area of British settlement began to grow.

Jamestown would soon see the first substantial Native-American–British conflict. That would be the start of what the winners called the "Indian Wars" and the losers called "the Conquest." In 1619 Jamestown would also see the first 20 African-American slaves arrive in British North America. They were the vanguard of what would become more than 4,400,000 African Americans by the time of the Civil War.

On the economic side Jamestown would also see the beginning of British tobacco cultivation on the North American mainland. Tobacco quickly became the colony's most important cash-producing crop by

The first permanent British settlement in Virginia, after three earlier colonizing attempts failed, was at Jamestown. This image shows the settlers landing at Jamestown in 1607.

One of the first tasks for new colonists was to build shelters. This usually involved cutting down trees to clear the land and also to provide fuel and wood for building.

far, beginning a pattern that strongly influenced the development of Virginia and other southern colonies.

John Rolfe, who later married Powhatan princess Pocahontas, was the key figure in the colony's successful cultivation of tobacco. He developed a variety of American tobacco that proved very attractive in Britain, making tobacco cultivation tremendously profitable. This attracted well-to-do planters, who founded large tobacco plantations on former Native-American land. Large numbers of farmers and poor farmworkers were also drawn to Virginia. Many originally came to America as bonded or indentured servants, working to pay off a debt, and then went west to become frontier farmers.

Virginia Wars

Tobacco cultivation also helped bring about the first British–Native-American war in North America. Some tobacco planters developed substantial tobacco-growing plantations on land taken from the Pamunkey people, part of the large Powhatan Confederacy. The Pamunkeys and the rest of the Powhatans had at first welcomed the British at Jamestown. They had supplied food to take the British through their first few years of settlement, literally a "starving time." Their chief, Powhatan (Wahunsunacock), was the father of Pocahontas and the brother of Opechancanough.

On Powhatan's death, probably in 1618, Opechancanough became leader of the Powhatans. Then what would become a very familiar and disastrous course of events began to play itself out. As the Jamestown colony grew, settlers took more and more Powhatan land, creating multiple incidents of British and Powhatan conflict. In 1622 the Powhatans made a surprise attack on the Jamestown colony, killing 350 settlers, or one-third of the entire population. That began the bitter First Virginia War (1622–1631), in which many Powhatan villages were destroyed and thousands of Powhatans killed or expelled.

In the following years the British became far stronger and occupied more of Virginia and much of what is now Maryland. In 1644 the remaining Powhatans attacked again, beginning the Second Virginia War (1644–1646). That war did not end in clear-cut British victory. However, as a practical matter it marked the end of the Powhatans and their neighbors, the Rappahannocks, both of whom lost their lands to continuing settler attacks. It also marked the effective end of this first set of Native-American wars of expulsion in British North America.

Opechancanough succeeded his brother, Powhatan, as chief of the Powhatan Confederacy. In 1622 he led a Native-American attempt to stop colonists from taking their lands, beginning the First Virginia War. Here he is shown after being captured by the Virginia colonists.

On the early frontier travelers either walked or—if they were lucky—rode horses, like this man on a road in early Maryland.

The British Expand

By the late 1660s the resisting Native-American peoples of the Virginia region were almost all gone, lost to war, epidemic disease, and expulsion from their homelands. That would be the main pattern of the Conquest—though later the forced expulsion of the Native-American nations from their homelands would become a matter of United States law, rather than occurring informally.

As would become common throughout British North America, the weakening of European colonial competition and the end of the Native-American nations brought much heavier British settlement to Virginia. This spurred development of frontier political and social life, education, and religion, and the rise of commerce and industry. This pattern would bring more than three centuries of continent-wide Native-American

This is a small frontier trading post dating from the 1600s at St. Mary's, in what is now Maryland.

wars, conquests, and expulsions to frontier America—and at the same time the rise of the new, continent-wide American nation.

By the 1670s the area of southern British settlement had grown to include the Tidewater—that is, the coastal regions of northern Virginia and much of Maryland—as well as the frontier regions leading to the foothills of the Appalachians. Substantial differences had grown between the Tidewater, dominated by the large tobacco planters, and the inland frontier regions, populated mostly by independent small farmers, trappers, and traders. By then there were tens of thousands of British settlers in Virginia and only a few thousand Native Americans left.

Frontier Rebellion

In the 1670s, a time of severe economic depression, the people of the frontier suffered from great hardship. They repeatedly clashed with the Native-American peoples of the area, whose land they wanted. They also clashed with the British colonial administration, which pursued a policy of peace with the Native Americans.

In 1676 British planter Nathaniel Bacon led a force of Virginia frontiersmen into a war aimed at destroy-ing the remaining Native-American peoples on the Virginia frontier. The war, first approved and then opposed by British colonial governor William Berkeley, quickly became an open armed conflict called

Parts of Jamestown were burned during Bacon's Rebellion in Virginia in 1676.

Bacon's Rebellion (1676–1677). Ultimately Bacon's forces took and burned Jamestown, the colonial capital. By 1677 the revolt was defeated by a strong force of British troops, and 23 of the rebels were executed. Bacon's Rebellion, the first in British-American colonial history, underscored the huge differences between the well-established and affluent parts of American society and the often rough people of the frontier, differences that would figure heavily in American history.

Throughout the colonial period Britain's Atlantic coast frontiers would continue to expand. They would come to form a solid front that, before the American Revolution, would start to move west to and through the Appalachians. After the Revolution the frontiers of the new United States would expand to take the nation west to the Pacific.

Later in the colonial period the British also moved south along the Atlantic coast. They overcame Spanish and some French opposition to plant colonies in the Carolinas in the 1670s and Georgia in the 1730s. The development of these British southern colonies would be greatly affected by the long set of European wars for North America that began in the late 1600s.

James Oglethorpe, founder of the British colony of Georgia, met here with the local Yamacraw people in the 1700s.

In their Mayflower Compact, signed while they were anchored off what would become Cape Cod's Provincetown, Pilgrims established the principle that all the men in the community were political equals—a principle extended to women only much later.

New England

In 1620, 13 years after Jamestown was established, British colonists opened a second major frontier region, this one in New England. In so doing, they also laid the basis for what became the second major set of Native-American wars and expulsions in British North America.

On December 26, 1620, the *Mayflower* arrived at Plymouth Harbor on Massachusetts Bay, carrying 101 Puritan colonists, called the Pilgrims. There they founded the second major British colony in North America, naming it New Plymouth after Plymouth, England.

The Pilgrims had set sail across the Atlantic from Plymouth on September 16, 1620. They had arrived at what is now Provincetown, on the tip of Cape Cod, on November 21, after spending more than two months at sea. They then spent more than a month exploring possible colony sites in the Massachusetts Bay area.

During their stay at Provincetown, the Pilgrims created the Mayflower Compact, one of the most basic and enduring documents of American democracy. The Compact declared all of the male colonists on the *Mayflower* to be politically equal. It was only a start, but for the time and place political equality was a radical notion indeed.

This idea would underlie much that came later, including the U.S. Constitution, the Bill of Rights, the end of slavery, and the rights of women and minorities.

The Pilgrims were English Protestants, part of the Puritan movement within the official English church, the Church of England. Puritans (including Pilgrims) were also called Dissenters, for they sharply disagreed with many Church of England practices. The main body of the Puritans fought for their beliefs within the Church of England. However, the Pilgrims disagreed so sharply that they seceded (withdrew) from that church, becoming a new "Separatist" movement. Facing tremendous persecution in England because of their secession, the Pilgrims fled to the Netherlands and then to North America, founding New Plymouth.

This is the *Mayflower II*, a modern reconstruction of the ship that carried the Pilgrims to the New World in 1620.

Plymouth Rock looms large as a symbol in North American history. However, it is really rather a small rock, as shown here, with the Mayflower at anchor in the background.

The landing of the Pilgrims at Plymouth, Massachusetts, has been a favorite subject for artists. This is a Nathaniel Currier view of that event.

The New Plymouth colony survived and slowly grew, though only with the help of the Wampanoags, part of the powerful Wampanoag Confederacy. The Wampanoags and their Native-American allies, including the Pequots, Narragansetts, and Nipmucks, controlled much of what today is New England. Sadly it was mostly their land that was taken by the New Plymouth and later Massachusetts Bay colonies.

Starting in the 1630s, large numbers of Puritans who had stayed in the Church of England followed the Pilgrims to North America. More than 24,000 Puritans emigrated to New England, in what came to be known as the Great Migration. These Puritans founded the Massachusetts Bay Colony, centered in Boston. From the mid-1600s on, this became the main center from which all of British New England grew.

Expanding Colonies

New England did grow—and fast. By the late 1600s the area of British settlement had grown to include large parts of southern New England, among them coastal areas from the Connecticut shore north to southern Maine. Inland New England was also fast being occupied, as colonists settled in large parts of the Connecticut River valley and inland areas of southern Massachusetts, both of which remained frontier areas.

The growth of New England put tremendous pressure on the Pequots and other New England Native Americans, who were pushed west and north out of their homelands. These Native Americans were largely peaceful farmers, fishers, and traders, as were the far stronger and more numerous British settlers who poured into their homelands.

Native-American–British relations, peaceful in the early years, soon gave way to armed clashes and then grew into wars. In the southern colonies British tobacco growers, seeking new lands for highly profitable tobacco, had led in the movement to take Native-American lands. In the northern colonies a flood of British farmers and frontier settlers just as surely moved to take Native-American lands. Their reasons may have been different from those of the southern British settlers, but the net effect was the same and would become a transcontinental pattern. Although Native Americans resisted, the incoming settlers were far too numerous, well organized, and well armed for their resistance to succeed.

British colonists quickly began to expand into interior New England. These Massachusetts families are traveling to the Connecticut River valley to settle Wethersfield and Windsor in what is now Connecticut, in the 1630s.

The Pequot War

In New England the first substantial "Indian War" was the Pequot War (1636–1637). Like the great majority of the American Indian Wars, its basic cause was the taking of Native-American homelands by frontier settlers. From the settlers' point of view, this was "empty" land, available for the taking to anyone who had the strength to hold it.

In this instance the Pequot homelands in southern Connecticut were invaded by British forces operating out of Boston and northern Connecticut. The British made a

The Pequot War, between the British colonists and the local Pequots, was notable for its violence. The colonists attacked and set fire to the main Pequot village, burning alive the people inside it and killing all those who tried to escape the fire. (The tipis shown here are an artist's invention, for these were not typical Native-American dwellings in New England.)

successful surprise attack on the main Pequot village, on the lower Connecticut River. They then surrounded and set fire to the village. With the extraordinary cruelty that was a shocking feature of many American Indian wars for more than 250 years, they burned the village and everyone in it—men, women, and children—killing anyone who tried to escape the flames. In all, 500 to 700 Pequots—the great majority of that branch of the Pequot nation—died in the attack.

King Philip's War

The second and by far the largest of the New England Indian Wars was King Philip's War (1675–1676). It was named after Wampanoag chief Metacom (King Philip to the British), the son of Massasoit, the Wampanoag chief who had done so much to help the Plymouth colony survive its early, difficult years.

By 1675 the British had put tremendous pressure on New England's Native Americans, who had also by then been greatly weakened by epidemic diseases brought to the Americas by European settlers. Large numbers of New England's remaining Native Americans had been forced into reservations, while others had fled west and north to other Native-American nations.

In 1675, after years of planning and alliance-building, Metacom led an alliance of Wampanoags, Nipmucks, and Narragansetts in a surprise armed revolt against the four British New England colonies—New Plymouth, Massachusetts Bay, Connecticut, and Rhode Island. More than half

Wampanoag chief Metacom, known to the British as King Philip, led Native-American forces during King Philip's War, the largest of the British–Native-American wars in New England.

of the New England settlements—most of them inland on the frontier—were attacked, though not most of the major coastal settlements. More than 600 settlers were killed and hundreds more wounded. Many of the frontier settlements were destroyed, their people driven out of the backcountry to the safety of the coastal settlements.

Yet the New England colonies were, by then, far stronger than the attacking Native-American forces. By the summer of 1676 Native-American forces had been largely defeated. In August of that year Metacom was killed in battle. In the end, Native-American losses were far larger than British ones, with far more dead and hundreds captured and sold into slavery. At war's end southern New England's Native Americans were expelled from their homelands, which were now occupied by the colonists. ❖

During King Philip's War the colonists most at risk of being attacked were those who lived on the frontier, as here with Native Americans attacking frontier farmers trying to bring in the harvest.

The first known Europeans to explore the Hudson River were English captain Henry Hudson and his Dutch party, sailing in the Half Moon in 1609. The event is shown here in a 19th-century painting by Albert Bierstadt.

New Netherland

During the colonial period, three other attacking European nations established North American frontiers. The first was the Netherlands. In 1609 English explorer Henry Hudson, leading a Dutch expedition, sailed into New York Harbor and went a considerable distance north on the Hudson River—then as now one of the greatest entryways into North America.

The Dutch returned to stay in 1612, establishing the New Netherland colony, a series of settlements on Manhattan Island (site of New Amsterdam, later to become New York City) and in the Hudson Valley.

Many were farming settlements, but those farther north were mainly fur-trading posts, often small forts. In 1614 the Dutch built Fort Orange, now Albany, which became the center of Dutch trade and power in the eastern Mohawk Valley.

The Dutch traded with many Native-American peoples and developed an alliance with the powerful Mohawks, part of the Iroquois Confederation. They actively supported the Mohawks in their major fur-trade wars of the period, supplying substantial amounts of guns, ammunition, and metal hand weapons such as axes and smaller hand axes called tomahawks. However, the Dutch did not fight side by side with their Native-American allies, as the French and British did. At the same time, Dutch relations with several of the Native-American peoples of the Hudson Valley were very poor, resulting in several major conflicts.

For the Dutch, as for other European colonial powers, North American power and position depended very heavily on the rise and fall of their fortunes in the never-ending European wars of the day. In the early 1600s the Protestant Netherlands had just completed its successful war of independence from Catholic Spain. This was at the same time part of a series of shifting alliances that involved all of the major European powers, in Europe and throughout the emerging colonial world. In South and East Asia the Dutch and their powerful navy fought a series of wars that won them dominance over the East Indies, later to

From the start the Dutch focused on trading with the Native Americans, rather than forming large colonies. Here Dutch fur traders are negotiating with Native Americans on Manhattan Island (now part of New York City).

This image shows a modest Dutch community—a blacksmith shop, farms, and a small shipyard—on Manhattan Island in the 1600s. Today this area is part of heavily populated New York City.

become Indonesia. In the Americas the Dutch fought a series of wars against competing European powers that left them very little power and territory in South and Central America, and none at all in North America.

There were three major British-Dutch wars in the 1600s, all of them involving the worldwide colonial ambitions of the two European powers. In 1664, while Britain and the Netherlands were fighting the undeclared war that would become the Second Anglo-Dutch War (1665–1667), a British fleet took and held New Amsterdam (September 7, 1664). Although the war ended in almost a draw, the British kept New Amsterdam and the whole New Netherland colony. They renamed the colony New York, while New Amsterdam became New York City.

During the Third Anglo-Dutch War (1672–1674) the Dutch retook New York. However, they returned the entire colony to Britain at the end of the war, effectively ending Dutch colonial presence in North America. New York went on to become one of the fastest-growing and economically strong of Britain's American colonies. ❖

This church and farmhouse are relics of the early Swedish settlement along the Delaware River in Pennsylvania.

New Sweden

Like the Netherlands, Sweden was a great European military power in the 1600s. And like the Netherlands and several other European powers, it set out to develop a colonial presence in the Americas.

In 1638 a force of 25 Swedish soldiers, aboard the *Kalmar Nyckel* and the *Fofel Grip*, sailed into the mouth of the Delaware River. There they built Fort Christina, a small fort at what is now Wilmington, Delaware, establishing what became Sweden's only colony in the Americas.

Further expeditions arrived during the 1640s and 1650s. These established other small fur-trading settlements in the Delaware River valley, in what are now Delaware, Maryland, New Jersey, and Pennsylvania.

Swedish territorial claims were large. However, New Sweden's population and power were small, for Sweden at home was involved in a series of massive European wars. It had little ability or inclination to build an American empire.

New Sweden—with a population of approximately 400 and competing with New Netherland in the fur trade—was no match for the Dutch fleet that sailed out of New Amsterdam against it in 1655. The Dutch took and held the colony, ending Swedish colonial ambitions in North America. ❖

The Pennsylvania Frontier

Like the most southern British coastal colonies in the Carolinas and Georgia, the growth of the Pennsylvania colony continued throughout the French-British war for North America. From the early 1700s through the American Revolution, colonists from earlier areas of settlement, as well as many coming directly from several European countries, continued to pour into Pennsylvania, New York, and the other mid-Atlantic colonies, making them by far the most heavily populated and commercially strong parts of British North America.

Despite its later importance, Pennsyl-

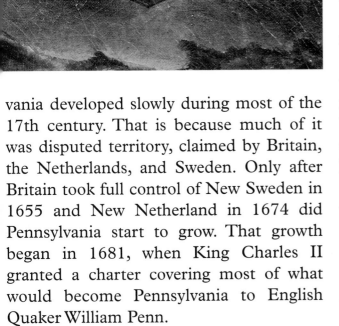

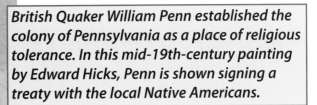
British Quaker William Penn established the colony of Pennsylvania as a place of religious tolerance. In this mid-19th-century painting by Edward Hicks, Penn is shown signing a treaty with the local Native Americans.

Penn then quickly moved to organize a colonial government, elect a colonial assembly, negotiate what turned out to be lasting and peaceful relations with the Native-American peoples of the region, and attract substantial numbers of colonists. Philadelphia, which would become one of the greatest cities of the new American nation, was founded in 1701. By the early 1700s a major new American frontier region had been established.

Pennsylvania, like New York, was a quite unusual British-American colony because of its diverse ethnic makeup. New England, Virginia, and most other northern and southern colonies were largely British. However, Pennsylvania, New York, and most of the other mid–Atlantic coast colonies were composed of several European ethnic groups. Two of the most important, especially on the frontiers, were the Scotch-Irish and the Germans. On their arrival in America, many of them went directly to the frontiers to find cheap land.

vania developed slowly during most of the 17th century. That is because much of it was disputed territory, claimed by Britain, the Netherlands, and Sweden. Only after Britain took full control of New Sweden in 1655 and New Netherland in 1674 did Pennsylvania start to grow. That growth began in 1681, when King Charles II granted a charter covering most of what would become Pennsylvania to English Quaker William Penn.

German Immigrants

Pennsylvania was the main destination of early German immigrants bound for America. Led by Francis Daniel Pretorius, the first organized group of German immigrants arrived in Pennsylvania aboard the *Concord* in 1683. They and other early arrivals founded Germantown, near Philadelphia. As large numbers of other German immigrants arrived by sea through Philadelphia, they went on to multiply and spread throughout Pennsylvania, moving south and east in the rich Delaware, Susquehanna, Lehigh, and Cumberland River valleys. Many other German immigrants went directly west to establish frontier settlements east of the Allegheny

Early German immigrants settled in Pennsylvania and many other British colonies along the East Coast. These are immigrants from Salzburg, Austria, arriving to settle in Georgia in 1733.

Mountains, part of the Appalachian Mountain chain that stretches from New England to Georgia. By the time of the American Revolution, German Americans formed an estimated one-third of the population of Pennsylvania and had settled throughout the frontier.

Large numbers of German Americans moved as far west as they could in British America, following the Great Valley of the Appalachians, which stretches southwest along the eastern slope of that mountain chain. As a result, they formed a major part of the frontier population of British America, from New York to Georgia. Others arrived by sea farther south, from Baltimore to Charleston, forming large German-American settlements throughout the mid-Atlantic and southern colonies.

While substantial numbers of Germans were going to Pennsylvania, other German immigrants—many of from the Palatine regions of Germany—were arriving in New York, drawn by British promises of jobs in the timber industry of the Hudson Valley. The promised jobs soon disappeared, but the immigrants remained. Many made their way to the New York frontiers, drawn by the fertile lands of the Hudson, Mohawk, and Schoharie River valleys. Other Palatine Germans migrated to Pennsylvania, Virginia, the Carolinas, and Georgia, in all forming another substantial portion of the frontier population.

Pioneers on the frontier were often protected by wooden forts enclosing small log cabins, as in this reconstruction of the 18th-century Fort Delaware on the Delaware River in Sullivan County, New York.

Scotch-Irish Immigrants

Even more numerous than the German Americans on the frontiers were the Scotch-Irish. Many Scotch-Irish immigrants went directly to the farthest British American frontiers, seeking land. They founded many frontier settlements, most of them on Native-American homelands.

Starting in the 1720s, large numbers of Scotch-Irish immigrants arrived at the port of Philadelphia. They quickly headed south and west, following the valleys on the eastern side of the Appalachians, creating pathways later named the Great Pennsylvania Wagon Road.

These frontier settlers played an extremely important role as American settlers burst through the Appalachians at Cumberland Gap on the Wilderness Road in the 1770s. They settled in the land beyond the mountains, including the Mississippi Valley, and created some of the main American ways west, finally going all the way to the Pacific.

Large numbers of other Scotch-Irish settlers went directly into western Pennsylvania. After the American Revolution they were a major part of the massive flood of settlers going west by way of Pittsburgh and the many waterways flowing into the Mississippi. Still other Scotch-Irish settlers followed the frontier south around the Appalachians and into the Deep South, Texas, and the Southwest.

When weather permitted, frontier people often did their cooking, washing, and other such chores near water, as here on the Susquehanna River in Pennsylvania.

Frontier Differences

Most Scotch-Irish immigrants were quite different from the Germans. Many Germans, such as the Mennonites, were religious pacifists who sought peaceful relations with the Native-American peoples they encountered. The Scotch-Irish and most other European immigrants had no such peaceful notions. Nor did the frontier Scotch-Irish easily go along with British colonial policies, which stressed alliances with Native-American peoples against the French in the long British-French war for North America.

From the first there was friction between the Scotch-Irish settlers and the British colonial governments. This would become even worse after the British victory over the French. In the 1760s American settlers and British forces had armed clashes in western Pennsylvania and other frontier regions.

From 1766 to 1771, during the run-up to the American Revolution, a continuing small-scale war existed on the North Carolina frontier between the "Regulators," a Scotch-Irish settlers' militia, and British troops. The war ended with the defeat of the Regulators at the Battle of Alamance and the execution of several militia leaders. Yet only four years later, in 1775, that small frontier war would become part of a much larger struggle—the American Revolution. ❖

All along the frontier, colonists were in conflict with Native Americans, as here on the Georgia and Carolina border.

Far northeastern Asia and far northwestern North America shared a land of ice and snow, lit at night by the strange and beautiful aurora borealis (northern lights), as in this 19th-century watercolor. Seals like the one in the foreground drew hunters from afar.

Russian America

The last of the European powers to open a North American frontier was Russia. In the mid-1700s it completed its long imperial journey all the way to Alaska.

For the Russians the way to the New World lay not west across the Atlantic, as it had for the British, French, Spanish, Dutch, and Swedes. Instead, the way lay east, far across Eurasia to the Pacific, and it took more than two centuries.

Russian fur traders and explorers began to move east and south across the Ural Mountain chain from Europe into Asia in the early 1500s. Russian military forces were quick to follow. In 1502 the Russian military defeated the Khanate of the Golden Horde, which since Mongol times had held much of southern Russia. That Russian victory fully opened the way across the Urals into Central Asia. By the 1520s

Among the many animals hunted for their fur in northern Asia and North America were sea otters. This old sea otter, no longer in much danger from hunters, rests on a beach.

Russian fur traders had moved much farther east, across the Amur River into Chinese-held Manchuria. Only 60 years later Russian forces began what became a very quick conquest of Siberia, opening much of northern Asia to Russian expansion.

By 1587 Russian settlers had followed, establishing the first Russian town in Siberia, at Tobolsk. This quickly became a center of Russian trade and settlement in the Russian Far East. The Russians then developed a network of forts, trading posts, and towns in Siberia, though the region remained lightly settled.

Still pursuing fur-bearing animals—

which, as in North America, were fast being destroyed by trappers and traders—the Russians reached the Pacific in 1638, establishing the town of Okhotsk. Five years later, in 1643, they reached Sakhalin Island, beginning a more than four-centuries-long dispute over ownership of the island, claimed by Japan. Another, far greater dispute began in 1651, when Russian forces reached the Amur River border with China. Military clashes and undeclared war quickly began in the Amur River region.

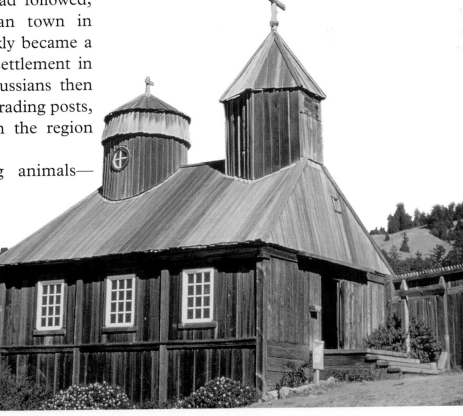
This wooden chapel was part of Fort Ross, Russia's outpost on the coast in northern California, originally called Fort Stawianski.

Alaska

Russian penetration of Alaska and the west coast of North America quickly followed, reaching as far south as northern California. In 1727 Vitus Bering, a Danish explorer leading a Russian expedition, discovered the waterway separating Alaska and the Aleutian Islands (at the northwestern tip of North America) from Asia. It was then named after him the Bering Strait. In 1741, leading another Russian expedition, Bering claimed the Aleutian Islands for Russia.

Russian exploration of the Aleutians and Alaska followed, but at no great speed. The newly discovered region was very far from

the centers of Russian population and power, and very far north, making both travel and trade difficult. Starting in the 1760s, Russian trappers and traders were active in the region, often clashing with such local Native-American peoples as the Aleuts, Yupiks, Tanainas, and Tlingits.

Many of the early Russians in the area treated these Native Americans with great brutality, killing many and enslaving many

Key Russian explorations of Alaska were led by Danish explorer Vitus Bering, who discovered Bering Strait, named for him. Here his 1741 expedition is being wrecked on the Aleutian Islands off Alaska, which he claimed for Russia.

others. Yet by far the greatest numbers of Native Americans were lost to the diseases brought by the Russians and other Europeans, as was so throughout the Americas.

The Russians established their first permanent North American settlement on Kodiak Island in 1784. Led by Alexander Baranov of the Russian American Company, they sharply increased their trading and settlement activities during the next 20 years in Alaska and as far south as northern California.

The Russians' second major American settlement was at Fort St. Michael, founded near modern Sitka in 1799. The Tlingit people attacked and destroyed Fort St. Michael in 1802, but it was resettled in 1804. Renamed New Archangel, it became the capital of Russian America. In 1812 the Russians established Fort Stawianski, a fur trading center in northern California. Later known as Fort Ross, it was completed two years later.

Although Russian America expanded in those years, Russia faced increasingly powerful opposition in North America. Weakening Spain could no longer oppose the Russians, but the United States and Britain were each far stronger than the Russians in North America.

In the mid-1820s Russia gave up most of its territorial claims south of Alaska, though keeping some trading rights. In 1841 the Russians sold Fort Ross to an American, John Sutter, leaving California. In 1867 the Russians withdrew from North America altogether, selling Alaska to the United States. ❖

From the earliest colonial days, European powers made alliances with some Native-American peoples as they set out to conquer others. In early Mexico, Spanish forces under Cortés made an alliance with the Tlaxcalas, here suing for peace, to defeat the Aztecs.

The Battle for North America

From very early in the European conquest of the Americas, all of the European nations involved were engaged in a very long body of declared and undeclared wars—against the Native-American peoples they were attacking and against each other. Often their wars against each other were in alliance with the very same Native-American peoples who were being conquered. One early example of European alliance-building was the Spanish–Native-American alliance against the Aztec Empire in the Valley of Mexico.

Nor was that kind of alliance-building confined to the Americas. Throughout the world, attacking Europeans took advantage of local enmities to divide and conquer, as the British did so notably in India, the European slavers in Africa, and the British, French, and Spanish in North America. The Dutch, Swedes, and Russians did the same. But, although these nations were powerful in other parts of the world, they had little influence on the course of events in North America.

Conflicts among the European nations

began in the Caribbean and spread to the North American mainland as a natural extension of the huge, complex set of imperial and religious wars rocking Europe and the growing colonial world. By the 1560s many British, French, Dutch, and other European pirates—some of them sponsored by their governments—were attacking Spanish gold and silver convoys in the Caribbean and the Atlantic. In the same period France, Britain, and Spain were fighting an undeclared war on the southeastern Atlantic coast, with Spain taking French Fort Caroline in 1565, and British pirate Francis Drake destroying Spanish St. Augustine in 1586.

Although Spain remained a major colonial power in the Americas all the way through the 1800s, it lost strength in North America even as Britain and France gained strength. During the North American colonial period, Spain suffered tremendous losses on what were its far northern borderlands. After the colonial period, Spain unsuccessfully tried to hold Mexico and to defend its remaining North American territories from the growing power of the new United States.

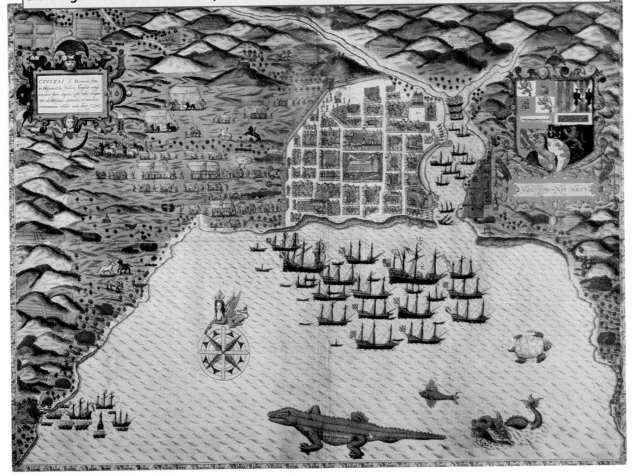

Throughout the Americas, European nations battled each other for riches and power. Here an English expedition under Francis Drake is attacking the Spanish settlement of Santo Domingo on the island of Hispaniola, in what is now the Dominican Republic.

One of the earliest and most important French settlements was at Port Royal in Acadia (later Nova Scotia), taken and destroyed by the British in 1613. It was rebuilt in modern times as a national historic site.

Britain and France

Farther north on the Atlantic coast, Britain and France soon entered what would become by far the most important European battle for North America. In 1609, only two years after establishment of Britain's Jamestown colony, British forces attacked French settlements in Acadia (later Nova Scotia). This began what would become more than a century and a half of declared and undeclared wars, most of them fought on the French and British colonial frontiers. Combatants included regular troops, provincial militia, trappers, traders, settlers, and their Native-American allies. For the Native Americans these were also often wars over who would dominate the fur trade, with the Iroquois on the British side, and most of the other Native-American peoples on the French side.

One of the earliest major battles of the 1600s was fought in Acadia in 1613, when British forces attacked and destroyed Port Royal (later Annapolis). During the British-French wars of the early 1630s, British forces also took Quebec and Acadia from the French. Yet, as would occur so often in

This is an interior room at the modern reconstruction of Port Royal.

the long conflict, the fate of the American territories was decided by what happened in Europe. Quebec and Acadia were returned to France in 1632 as part of a European peace treaty. That would happen again in 1670, when Acadia was returned to France under the 1667 Treaty of Breda, which ended the Second Anglo-Dutch War.

King William's War

Three more major European wars, one of them a massive world war, also played roles in deciding the fate of North America. The first, called King William's War (1689–1697) in North America, was part of Europe's War of the League of Augsburg. This war involved Britain, France, Spain, the Netherlands, and several other countries. In North America, it was a long, hard-fought colonial war, fought largely on the French and British frontiers. The British again took Acadia, and they raided into New France. However, it was the British frontier settlements that bore the weight of the main fighting, as the French and their Native-American allies made continuing attacks on British frontier settlements all the way from Maine to New York. In the end, the peace treaty ending the war mainly restored prewar North American borders.

During King William's War in the winter of 1689–1690, French and allied Native-American forces attacked many frontier settlements, as here in Schenectady, New York.

One of the greatest massacres in the long series of French-British wars occurred in 1689 at the village of Lachine, near Montreal. There more than 200 French settlers were killed by attacking Mohawks, allies of the British. In the same period hundreds of British settlers were killed by French and allied Native-American raiders at Portland (then Casco Bay), Maine; Schenectady, New York; and scores of other frontier settlements.

Queen Anne's War

A second European war with tremendous impact on the American frontier quickly followed. This was the War of the Spanish Succession (1701–1714), in North America called Queen Anne's War (1702–1713). The North American part of the war involved France, Britain, Spain, and their Native-American allies. It was fought mainly on the frontiers, from Florida and the Gulf Coast all the way north into New France.

In the north, where the main military actions of the war were fought, British and allied Native-American forces took Port Royal. However, in by far the largest single action of the war in North America, they failed to take Quebec and Montreal, after a British invasion fleet was destroyed in bad weather on the St. Lawrence, with the loss of almost 1,000 men.

Yet it was in the South that the most important actions of the war took place. There Carolina militia forces and their Native-American allies, mostly Yamasees, developed the long series of attacks that would, in the end, drive many southern Native-American peoples from their home-lands. One of the major southern wars of expulsion was the Tuscarora War (1711–1713), in which almost 1,000 Tuscaroras were killed and 400 captured, almost destroying the Tuscarora nation. Of these almost 600 were killed and 400 captured when Carolina raiders and their Native-American allies burned the main Tuscarora village at Fort Nohoroco, North Carolina. Most of the remaining Tuscaroras fled north to New York, where they became the sixth nation in the Iroquois Confederation.

Britain and Spain were on opposite sides in many European wars. Here British forces from the colony of Georgia are attacking Spain's Florida territories.

Queen Anne's War was ended in Europe in 1713 by the Treaty of Utrecht, in which Britain won Acadia, Hudson Bay, and Newfoundland. Although the war formally ended, the long war continued on the French, British, and Spanish North American frontiers.

In a bitter aftermath to Queen Anne's War, British settlers and traders continued to attack Native Americans in the Carolinas. This resulted in the Yamasee War (1715–1718), a war of expulsion by the British against their former allies, the Yamasees.

Though no formal war immediately followed Queen Anne's War, neither was there peace on the frontiers. In the North, France and Britain continued to fight a bitter frontier war. In the South, border wars continued, involving Britain, France, Spain, and many Native-American peoples.

As settlers expanded on the frontier, surveyors were brought in to lay out land claims. These two surveyors on the Carolina frontier were captured by the local Tuscaroras during Queen Anne's War.

King George's War

The French and British in North America were involved in yet another European war in the 1740s. This was King George's War (1744–1748), a very small part of Europe's massive War of the Austrian Succession.

In the main action of the war, British provincial forces took the great French fortress at Louisbourg, in Acadia (later Nova Scotia). Once again the British were forced to return it as part of the peace treaty ending the war. ❖

The great French fort at Louisbourg in Acadia (later Nova Scotia) changed hands several times during the colonial wars. It was later destroyed and then reconstructed as a historic site, today "guarded" by soldiers in 18th-century dress.

Stretching into the distance over the narrow mountain pathway, a long line of British soldiers under General Braddock is marching to attack France's Fort Duquesne (later Pittsburgh).

The French and Indian War

The fate of New France and British America was finally settled by one more European war, the massive world war called the Seven Years War (1756–1763). In North America the war started earlier, in 1754, and was known as the French and Indian War (1754–1763).

In Europe the Seven Years War pitted France, Austria, Russia, Sweden, and Saxony against Prussia and Britain. It generated huge battles between the forces of the two groups of powers, with armies sometimes totaling hundreds of thousands and casualties running into the tens of thousands. Yet it was an indecisive war in Europe, ending in a draw, with national borders largely restored to their prewar boundaries.

The war turned out very differently in the colonial world. There it was mainly a major struggle between Britain and France, with Spain and several other European colonial powers playing smaller roles. Outside Europe the Seven Years War was

One of the key forts on the French frontier was Fort Duquesne, at what is now Pittsburgh, where the Monongahela and Allegheny Rivers join to form the Ohio River, as shown in this 19th-century painting by Frank Earle Schoonover.

fought in the Americas, Asia, and Africa, and on most of the world's major oceans, being at least as much a naval war as it was a land war. For the European colonial powers, its great prizes were India and North America, though other very substantial prizes were also won. In the end, the colonial part of the Seven Years War was not at all a draw. Rather, it was a huge set of victories for Britain over France, with Britain driving France out of India and the North American mainland.

War on the Frontier

For the people of the American frontier, the French and Indian War was a long, bitterly fought extension of the murderous border wars between the French, British, and Native Americans, which had by then been going on for almost a century and a half. Nor would those wars end with British victory in the French and Indian War, for the American Revolution and the War of 1812 still lay ahead. The long American frontier wars would continue for more than another half century, then pitting the

BEFORE THE FRENCH AND INDIAN WAR.

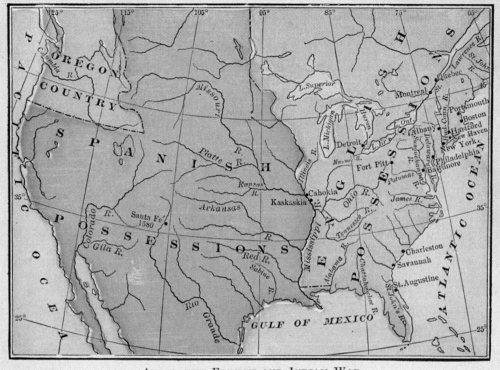

AFTER THE FRENCH AND INDIAN WAR.

The North American Colonies before and after the French and Indian War
These two maps of European possessions in North America before and after the Treaty of Paris in 1763 show Britain as a major winner in the colonial game. Spain also made huge gains on paper, but never effectively occupied or held most of the territory it claimed.

British and their Native-American allies against the new American nation.

The French and Indian War began in the Ohio Valley, on what was then the northwestern frontier. It started with a confrontation between Virginia militia led by Colonel George Washington and much stronger French and Native-American forces out of nearby Fort Duquesne (later Pittsburgh). After a brief engagement, Washington surrendered to the French and received safe conduct out of French territory.

Washington's colonial forces returned in 1755 as part of British general Edward Braddock's forces. They suffered a disastrous defeat by French and Indian forces on the Monongahela River near Fort Duquesne. In the same year British forces expelled most of the French-speaking people of Acadia (Nova Scotia), many of whom then settled in French-speaking Louisiana.

The rest of the French and Indian War was fought primarily in what are now eastern Canada and the northeastern United States. Early in the war French and Native-American forces scored several substantial

Fighting for the British during the French and Indian War, George Washington gained experience he would use during the American Revolution. Here Washington is on a mission to the Ohio River.

victories, and throughout the war they successfully attacked British frontier settlements. In the end, however, superior British naval forces and combined British and colonial land forces proved too strong for the French and their Native-American allies. In 1758 British and American forces took the great French fortress at Louisbourg, Nova Scotia. In the west they also took Fort Duquesne and several other French fortresses, including Fort Frontenac, on Lake Ontario. The final major battle of the war came in 1759, when the British took the French fortress at Quebec, effectively ending the war.

The Treaty of Paris—which formally ended the worldwide colonial portion of the war, including the war in North America—was signed in 1763. Under that treaty all of what had been French Canada went to Britain, as did Florida and all former French territories east of the Mississippi River, except New Orleans. Spain took New Orleans and western Louisiana.❖

European treaties may have settled world wars, but all along the frontier settlers continued to be at war with Native Americans. These settlers in colonial South Carolina carried their rifles on their backs even as they worked their fields.

Set Index

Figures in bold are the volume numbers; the other figures are the page numbers.